LIVES AND TIMES

Bach

Wendy Lynch

Heinemann
LIBRARY

First published in Great Britain by Heinemann Library,
Halley Court, Jordan Hill, Oxford OX2 8EJ,
a division of Reed Educational and Professional Publishing Ltd.
Heinemann is a registered trademark of Reed Educational & Professional Publishing Limited.

OXFORD MELBOURNE AUCKLAND
JOHANNESBURG BLANTYRE GABORONE
IBADAN PORTSMOUTH NH (USA) CHICAGO

Designed by Visual Image
Illustrations by Sally Barton
Originated by Dot Gradations
Printed and bound in Hong Kong/China

05 04 03 02 01
10 9 8 7 6 5 4 3 2 1

ISBN 0 431 02313 1
This title is also available in a hardback library edition (ISBN 0 431 02306 9)

British Library Cataloguing in Publication Data

Lynch, Wendy
Bach. – (Lives and times)
1. Bach, Johann Sebastian, 1685–1750 – Juvenile literature
2. Composers – Germany – Biography – Juvenile literature
I. Title
780.9'2
ISBN 0431023131

Acknowledgements

The Publishers would like to thank the following for permission to reproduce photographs: AKG London: pp16, 17, 18, 22, 23; Mary Evans Picture Library: p19; NASA/Science Photo Library: p21; Yiorgos Nikiteas: p21.

Cover photograph reproduced with permission of e.t. archive.

Every effort has been made to contact copyright holders of any material reproduced in this book. Any omissions will be rectified in subsequent printings if notice is given to the Publisher.

For more information about Heinemann Library books, or to order, please phone ++44 (0)1865 888066, or send a fax to ++44 (0)1865 314091. You can visit our website at www.heinemann.co.uk.

Any words appearing in the text in bold, **like this**, are explained in the Glossary.

Contents

Early life

Johann Sebastian Bach was born in Germany on 21 March 1685. Bach's father taught him to play the violin and viola as soon as his hands were big enough.

Bach started going to school when he was seven years old. He learnt **Latin**, History and Maths. Bach also sang in a **choir** in church.

Bach the organist

When Bach was ten, both his parents died. He went to live with his oldest brother. His brother taught him to play the organ and to make up his own music. This is called **composing**.

Bach was a **brilliant** organ player. His little finger was as strong as his **index finger** and could move as fast. This meant he could play fast music without making a mistake.

Patrons

When Bach was eighteen, he began to earn money by playing music. He began **composing** and playing music for rich and important people. These people were called **patrons**.

Bach's first patron was a duke. For the Duke's birthday, Bach wrote a piece of music called 'Sheep May Safely **Graze**'. This music was written with words so that it could be sung.

Marriage

Bach married his cousin Maria Barbara in 1707. They had seven children, but three of them died. Bach wrote a book of music for them called *The Little Organ Book*.

In 1717, Bach began to work for another **patron**, called Prince Leopold. The Prince loved music and he gave Bach and his family rooms in his palace.

Family and music

In 1720 Bach's wife Maria Barbara died suddenly. In 1722 Bach married Anna Magdalena. They went on to have thirteen children, but seven of them died when they were young.

Bach became head of a music school.
Bach and his students played **concerts** in
cafés. Bach wrote the 'Coffee **Cantata**'
for one of these concerts.

Playing for the King

In 1741 Bach visited the palace of King Frederick in Berlin, Germany. Bach played for the King and later wrote some music specially for him.

By 1750, Bach was not doing much work because he could not see very well. Bach died on 28 July 1750. He was 65 years old.

Buildings from Bach's time

We can visit the house where Bach was born. Now it is a museum. In the house you can see the musical instruments Bach played when he was a boy.

You can visit the church in Leipzig, Germany, where Bach used to play the organ. Bach was buried here after he died.

Letters and music

We can still read Bach's letters today.
This letter was written on 28 October
1730, when Bach was 45 years old.

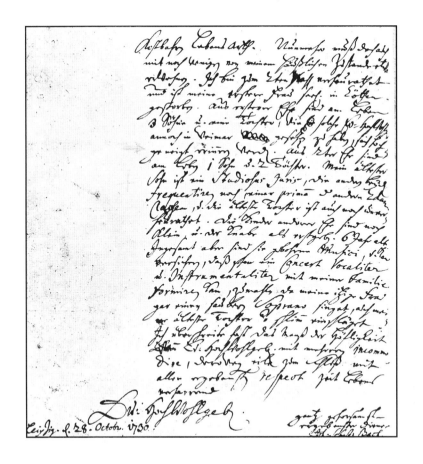

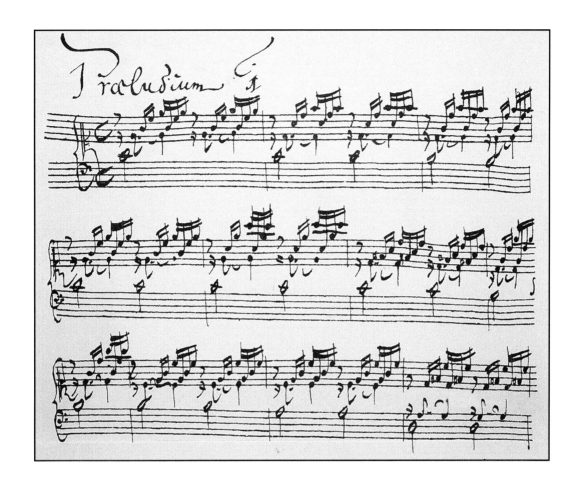

Here is a **manuscript** written by Bach.
It shows how he wrote music on a page.
When Bach was alive all music had to
be written by hand.

Concerts and CDs

You can listen to Bach's music on a CD or on the radio. This is a CD of Bach's *Brandenburg* **Concertos**.

When the Voyager spacecraft set off into space in 1977, a **recording** of Bach's *Brandenburg Concertos* was put inside it. If there was life on another planet, people there could hear Bach's music.

Paintings and statues

Paintings show us what Bach looked like.
This one was painted when Bach was
35 years old.

You can still see this statue in memory of
Bach in Eisenach, Germany. He is holding
some music. The statue shows us that
Bach and his music are still remembered.

Glossary

This glossary explains difficult words, and helps you to say words which may be hard to say.

brilliant someone who is very, very good at doing something. You say *bril-ee-ant*.

cantata a short piece of music for voice and instruments. You say *can-tar-ta*.

choir group of singers. You say *kw-ire*.

compose make up music

concert public show by musicians or singers. You say *kon-sert*.

concerto piece of music in three parts, often for one instrument and an orchestra. You say *con-cher-toe*.

graze the way cows and sheep feed

index finger finger you point with, next to your thumb

Latin people who lived in ancient Rome spoke Latin

manuscript music written by hand. You say *man-you-script*.

patron someone who gives money and support to a person or group. You say *pay-tron*.

recording piece of music stored on tape or disc. You say *rek-aw-ding*.

Index